GET ACTIVE!

BAT AND BALL SPORTS

Barbara C. Bourassa

First published in the UK in 2007 by
QED Publishing
A Quarto Group company
226 City Road
London EC1V 2TT
www.qed-publishing.co.uk

A catalogue record for this book is available from the British Library.

ISBN 978 1 84538 651 1

Written by Barbara C. Bourassa
Edited, designed and picture researched by
  Starry Dog Books Ltd
Consultant Steven Downes, of the Sports Journalists'
  Association www.sportsjournalists.co.uk

Publisher Steve Evans
Creative Director Zeta Davies
Senior Editor Hannah Ray

Printed and bound in China

Website information is correct at time of going to press. However, the publishers cannot accept liability for any information or links found on third-party websites.

All the sports in this book involve differing degrees of difficulty and the publisher would strongly advise that none of the activities mentioned are undertaken without adult supervision or the guidance of a professional coach.

Words in **bold** can be found in the Glossary on pages 30–31.

Picture credits
Key:
T = top, B = bottom, C = centre, L = left, R = right, FC = front cover, BC = back cover

S = Shutterstock.com, C = Corbis, D = Dreamstime.com, G = Getty Images, BSP = Big Stock Photo.com, ISP = iStockphoto.com

Credits:
FC (main image) G/ © Jim Cummins, (top to bottom) S/ © SI, S/ © Alexander Kalina, S/ © Glenda M. Powers, S/ © Alan C. Heison, S/ © Larry St. Pierre, S/ © MAT, S/ © Steve Cukrov.

1 S/ © Sonya Etchison; 4 S/ © Alan C. Heison; 5 (top to bottom) S/ © MAT, S/ © SI, S/ © Alexander Kalina, S/ © John Barry de Nicola; 6t C/ © Michael St. Maur Sheil, 6b C/ © Nik Wheeler; 7 C/ © Royalty-Free; 8t S/ © Graca Victoria, 8b S/ © Phil Anthony; 9 D/ © Freefly; 10t S/ © Lance Bellers, 10bl S/ © Jason Merideth; 11 G/ © Jim Cummins; 12b C/ © Liu Liqun; 13c C/ © Mark Gamba, 13bl ©2007 ITTF Museum, all rights reserved, www.ittf.com/museum; 14bl S/ © Lori Carpenter; 15 C/ © Brownie Harris; 16c C/ © Bettmann, 16bl S/ © Andrea Catenaro Doherty; 17 S/ © Larry St. Pierre; 18t Skijornow.com/ R. Briggle, 18bl S/ © James M Phelps, Jr; 19 D/ © Christophriddle; 20t D/ © Webking, 20b S/ © Steve Cukrov; 21cl D/ © Christophriddle, 21cr S/ Riddle Photography; 22t C/ © Reuters, 22b S/ © Alexander Kalina; 23tl D/ © Dshawley, 23c C/ © Eliana Aponte/Reuters; 24 C/ © Ariel Skelley; 25bl S/ © Norliza binti Azman, 25c D/ © Slinscot; 26t S/ © Kamarulzaman Russali, 26b ISP/ © Lance Bellers Photography; 27 C/ © Roy McMahon; 28t ISP/ © Uzinusa, 28b C/ © Royalty-Free; 29 G/ Stockbyte.

BC S/ © Peter Weber.

CONTENTS

IN THE world of sport, there are many different activities that use some type of bat (or stick) and ball. You might choose to hit tennis balls over a net with a racquet, or you may fancy learning how to pot balls with a pool cue. There's a bat and ball sport to suit every personality!

Plenty of choice

If you like playing in a team, consider lacrosse or hockey. If you prefer an individual sport, tennis may be the game for you. If you like fast action, try table tennis. If a slower pace, with sudden spurts of activity, is more your style, you could try baseball. Whatever sport you chose, they are all fun, easy to learn and a great way to make new friends!

➡ *Some female lacrosse players wear cage-like face guards to protect their eyes during a game.*

TIME AND PATIENCE

Before you set off for the field, court or pitch, there are a number of things to keep in mind. Remember that many of the players you see on the television or at live events are professional players with years of experience (and practice). So don't expect to be as good as they are straight away! Learning any new sport takes time and patience, and it's best to focus first on having fun, rather than trying to master every little detail of your chosen sport.

Protect yourself

Many bat and ball sports require protective gear for the body or face, such as helmets and pads. Lacrosse players, for instance, usually wear heavy padded gloves to protect their hands, and most cricket players wear helmets and pads. Such protective equipment for your head and body can prevent injuries if you bump into another player, are hit by a ball or slip and fall down.

Practice makes perfect

As any good **coach** will tell you, learning a new sport means understanding and mastering the basics. You'll need to look after your equipment carefully, and get plenty of practice. All sports, from golf to table tennis, keep you healthy and active. Remember to drink plenty of water, eat well and take breaks whenever you need to. Most sports also involve a certain amount of danger. But when they are played correctly, they're all fun, so turn the page for the low-down on some top bat and ball sports!

LACROSSE

LACROSSE is an exciting game that was invented by First Nations/Native Americans. The modern game is played by two teams of 10 (men) or 12 (women). The players use lacrosse sticks, called crosses, to move a hard rubber ball around a field. They use the net-like pockets at the ends of their sticks to scoop the ball off the ground and pass it to other players, who catch it and pass it on using their sticks.

Aim of the game

Lacrosse is similar to football in that the players run back and forth trying to get the ball into the other team's goal. The attackers line up close to the opponent's goal and try to score. The defenders stay near their own goal to defend it from the other team's attackers. As in football, each team's goalkeeper stays close to his or her goal to guard it from the other team's players.

WHAT IS HURLING?

Hurling is thought to be the oldest field game in Europe. It is an Irish game similar to lacrosse. The stick (or hurley) and ball (or sliothar) resemble those used in hockey. Two teams of 15 players hit the ball on the ground or in the air, and a player can pick up the ball with his or her stick and carry it for four steps.

Lacrosse on horseback

Polocrosse is a sport that combines lacrosse and **polo**. Players carry sticks that resemble lacrosse sticks, but they ride ponies as in a game of polo.

◀ In polocrosse, two teams of six players play the game on horseback.

Protective gear

Lacrosse players wear helmets to protect their heads, and on their hands they wear large, padded gloves. There's a lot of running involved, so if you want to try lacrosse, get ready to work your leg muscles!

➤ *The French named the early lacrosse sticks 'crosses', because they looked like a bishop's crozier or staff, called a 'crosse'.*

DID YOU KNOW?

Lacrosse is played at international level by 26 countries and the Iroquois Nationals. The Iroquois is a group of First Nations/ Native Americans mainly from eastern Canada and the northeast of the USA. They are the only First Nations/Native American team that competes in international sport.

LEARN MORE

Visit these lacrosse-related web sites:
• www.bbc.co. uk/cbbc/sport/ findasport/lacrosse. shtml
• www.laxlinks.com

TENNIS

TENNIS is fun and easy to learn. All you need to play is a racquet, a ball, a net to hit the ball over and someone to play against. A large, rectangular court is generally used, either indoors or outdoors.

What to wear

It used to be that tennis clothing had to be white, white and whiter. Today, however, tennis outfits have changed. It's not unusual to find tennis players wearing red, blue, pink or even black outfits.

TENNIS TALK

You will need to buy, rent or borrow a tennis racquet if you want to play tennis. The 'grip' is the area of the tennis racquet that you hold on to, or grip. The 'head' is the part of the racquet that hits the ball. Strings across the head form a grid of netting off which the ball bounces.

Who's who in tennis

Because tennis is so popular, its best players are often well known to many people. In the United States, for instance, Serena Williams is widely recognized. Roger Federer of Switzerland is a multiple winner at the major competitions of Wimbledon and the US **Open**. Among female tennis players, Maria Sharapova of Russia, Amelie Mauresmo of France and Kim Clijsters of Belgium have many loyal fans.

◀ Maria Sharapova was born on 19 April 1987 in Siberia, Russia. She is 1.82m tall, and is one of the world's best tennis players.

Where to play

If you want to learn tennis, there are many ways to do so, from group or individual lessons to tennis camp or tennis clubs. Tennis can be played outdoors on **asphalt**, clay or grass courts, or indoors at a sports centre. In some parts of the world, outdoor tennis courts are roofed over in the winter with stiff domes of plastic called bubbles so players can play all year round.

➤ *Tennis is often played in the summer on outdoor courts. Players wear shorts or short skirts and lightweight shirts to keep cool.*

FAMOUS COMPETITIONS

Tennis is popular all over the world, and many people like to follow the game (and the players) by attending competitions such as the US Open, the French Open or the Australian Open. If you can't get to a live event, you can follow the action on television. During the two weeks of the summer when Wimbledon is shown on TV, the streets often seem much emptier!

Singles and doubles

In tennis there are two main types of play. In a singles game there are just two players, one on each side of the net. In a doubles game there are four players on the tennis court, a team of two (called a pair) on each side of the net. In both types of game, only one ball is hit back and forth. The court is marked with outer sidelines and inner sidelines. Doubles players can hit the ball to the outer lines and singles players use the inner ones.

Racquetball and squash

The games of squash and racquetball are related to tennis. Both involve hitting a rubber ball around an indoor court. In tennis, if the ball is hit outside the court it is considered out of bounds, but in racquetball and squash you can hit the ball off the walls, as well as the floor. Both squash and racquetball can be played as a singles game or a doubles game.

GAMES	POINTS
3	30
2	40

GAME, SET, MATCH

The scoring system in tennis is quite complicated. Tennis is played in a sequence of **games** that are scored using points. Several games (usually at least six) make up a **set**, and generally two or three sets (but it can be as many as five) make up a **match**.

◀ A racquetball is slightly larger than a squash ball, and the racquet has a shorter handle.

BADMINTON BASICS

Badminton is similar to tennis, but everything is a different shape! The racquets are lighter, the court is smaller, the net is taller, and instead of hitting a ball back and forth, players hit a small cone called a 'shuttlecock' or 'bird'. Badminton became an Olympic sport in 1992, when Indonesia, South Korea and China won most of the medals.

Try, try and try again...

If you are learning tennis, you will probably do lots of practice exercises, designed to help improve your skills. Your coach may stand close to the net, for instance, and send over practice balls for you to return. Another easy way to practise tennis is to hit the ball against a wall.

OLYMPIC TENNIS

At the 2004 Olympic Games in Athens, China won its first gold medal in tennis. Li Ting and Sun Tiantian beat a pair (team) from Spain for the top honours in the women's doubles.

Stop and start

Tennis is a game of movement. Because the ball can be hit anywhere on the court, you'll need to run after it. Learning to run after the ball and then slow down enough to hit it back over the net can take some practice.

▶ *When serving, the player stands behind the baseline, throws the ball up into the air and hits it over the net into the service box diagonally opposite (marked by white lines on the ground).*

TABLE TENNIS

TABLE TENNIS is a fast and exciting game in which two players use small bats to hit a hard plastic ball over a low net strung across a table. The players take it in turns to serve for two points in a row. The first player to get 11 points (with a two-point lead) wins the game. When the server strikes, the ball must bounce on the server's side of the net first and then on the opponent's side before it is returned. The game requires great speed, and is fun both to watch and play!

DID YOU KNOW?

Table tennis has very precise rules. According to the International Table Tennis Federation (ITTF), an official table tennis ball must be white or orange and weigh 2.7g.

◆ Ping-pong is a popular sport with children all over China. These schoolchildren from the Guangxi Zhuangzu region are playing on a table made from a piece of concrete and a line of bricks.

▶ World champion table tennis players come from all over the world. Many of the world's best players are from China and South Korea.

What is ping-pong?

Ping-pong is an affectionate name for table tennis. It is the term generally used when the game is played just for fun by children. Most people agree that the name came from the 'ping' and 'pong' noise made by the ball in the days before bats had foam cushions.

Getting started

To get started in table tennis you will need a few basic pieces of equipment: a table tennis bat (also called a paddle or racquet in the USA), a ball, a net and a table. In international competitions the net must rise exactly 15.25cm above the table. At home you don't need to be so precise. Instead of a net you could use string, a piece of fabric or even a row of tin cans!

DID YOU KNOW?

In Switzerland there is a museum of table tennis (see www.ittf.com/museum/). Why not try out its simulated game on your computer? Check it out at: http://www.ittf.com/games/game.htm

BASEBALL is a very American game. To get a game going, you will need only a ball, a bat and a few friends to play with. You might also want a glove for catching the ball and a cap for keeping the sun out of your eyes.

GET YOUR GLOVE

Baseball gloves come in many different types. It's important to buy the right kind of glove for the position you are playing. If you are just getting started, you'll need a basic fielder's glove for catching.

Pitcher and catcher

In an organized game of baseball, two teams of nine players take turns to bat. The game starts when the **pitcher** throws the ball to the **catcher**. The catcher crouches behind the **home plate**, one of four **bases** on the field. The other team's batter, standing in a marked area on one side of the home plate, attempts to hit the ball so that he can run around the four bases and score **runs**.

Scoring runs

If the batter hits the ball, he or she must run to first base (the batter becomes a **runner**). The batter can either stop there, or run on to the next base. If the batter runs from first to second to third base and back to the home plate without stopping and without being got **out**, he or she scores a **home run**. The team with the most runs wins.

◄ Before taking a swing at the ball, the batter holds the bat at a 45 degree angle over the back shoulder. He or she must also keep both eyes on the ball.

The four bases

The main square area of the field in which a game takes place is called the diamond. In the centre is the pitcher's mound, where the pitcher stands to throw the ball to the catcher. The corners of the diamond are marked by the four bases. Each base is guarded by a **fielder** called a **baseman**, who is ready to catch the ball.

DID YOU KNOW?

Baseball is thought to have developed in the mid 1700s from the English game of **rounders**. In rounders, two teams of nine players take turns batting and fielding the ball. The batter scores a 'rounder' by running past each post before the other team's fielders can 'tag' or touch the posts with the ball.

➡ This baseball game is being held at the Rogers Centre in Toronto, Canada. The stadium is unusual in having a huge roof that can open and close over the whole ground. It seats 51,517 fans at baseball games.

Fielding positions

In an organized game, there are nine fielders on the field at any one time. These include the pitcher and catcher, then first baseman, second baseman, third baseman and short stop (who fields between second and third base). Outside the diamond, at the greatest distance from the batter, are the left fielder, centre fielder and right fielder. The fielders must be good at catching and throwing the ball.

Girls and baseball

Although many people think baseball is a male sport, plenty of girls like to play, too. In many parts of the USA, 10- to 12-year-old girls play alongside boys on their baseball teams. Some girls also like **softball**, a game similar to baseball but which uses a larger ball.

➤ *You can take a tour or even have a birthday party at Yankee Stadium, home of the New York Yankees.*

Starting young

In the USA, children aged four or five might play T-ball, a game in which you hit the ball off a T-shaped stand. Older children can move on to play baseball and softball games organized by the **Little League**.

World-famous Yankees

The New York Yankees are probably the best-known baseball team in the world. The reason? They have won the **World Series** 26 times! The World Series is a competition between the winners of the two leagues that make up **Major League Baseball** in the USA and Canada.

Worldwide appeal

Many baseball players from all over the world go to the USA to play. The Dominican Republic, Cuba, Japan and Puerto Rico are all well known for their baseball stars. On the streets of the Dominican Republic, children play baseball almost all year round. One of the most famous players in Major League baseball is Sammy Sosa, from the Dominican Republic.

COOPERSTOWN

The US Baseball Hall of Fame is in New York State. Taking a trip to Cooperstown to learn about famous baseball players such as Babe Ruth, Ted Williams and Joe DiMaggio (left) is a fun adventure for many children (and their parents!). You can visit the hall of fame online at www.baseballhalloffame.org

When batting, baseball players wear helmets to protect their heads. They also wear shoes with studs, which give good grip when they are running.

GOLF

THE GAME of golf involves using various clubs to hit a small ball along a course and into a set of 18 small holes. Along the way are obstacles such as lakes, sand pits (bunkers), trees and rough grass. The player who hits his or her ball into the 18 holes using the smallest number of hits (or strokes) wins.

Talented Tiger

Tiger Woods is one of the world's best players. He has won many major golf tournaments, including the **Masters** four times, the British Open three times and the US Open twice.

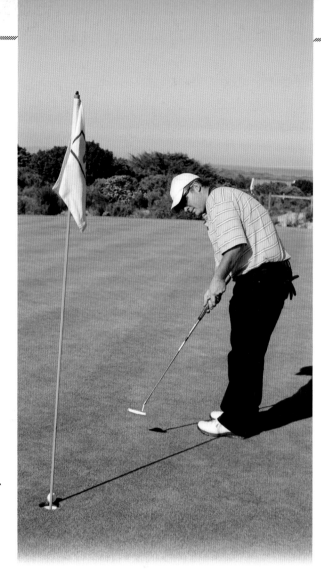

→ *This man has just hit his golf ball towards a hole using a **putter**.*

→ *Tiger Woods (USA) started playing golf at the age of two. He hit his first **hole-in-one** at the age of six.*

GOLF CLUBS

Golf players carry a range of clubs, each one designed for a different use. Most clubs can be grouped into one of three categories: **woods**, **irons** or putters.

Which club to use?

A player starts a game by hitting the ball for a long distance from a special area of the course called the **tee**. To hit long distances, most people use a club called a 'wood' or 'driver'. The driver has a large, rounded head designed to push the ball as far as possible along the course. As the player gets closer to the hole, he or she will probably use clubs called 'irons'. These tend not to hit the ball as far as woods, but are used for more accurate shots. Once the ball is on the green – an area of very short grass where the hole is located – the player uses a 'putter' to hit the ball into the hole.

WELL-KNOWN WOMEN GOLFERS

Golf is a great game for girls, some of whom go on to become top-earning professional women golfers. Michelle Wie of the USA did so when she was just 15 years old. Two other world-famous women golfers are Annika Sorenstam of Sweden and Lorena Ochoa of Mexico.

◄ Many golfers wear a glove on one hand to help them grip their clubs.

Worldwide appeal

Golf has been played for at least 500 years in the UK, though its origins are uncertain. Today it is played all over the world, on courses that try to use the natural environment – streams, lakes, hills and trees – to add difficulty to the golfer's game. But it can be played anywhere. It was even played on the Moon, where astronaut Alan Shepard on lunar mission Apollo 14 played a shot that he said went for "miles and miles" because of the low gravity!

Miniature golf, also called crazy golf, is a popular pastime with tourists at seaside resorts.

Miniature golf

Young children may enjoy miniature golf. The player uses a putter to move the ball through and around various obstacles – such as model bridges – in as few strokes as possible.

Where to learn golf

There are many places to learn golf. Many large golf courses offer junior lessons. There are also golf clubs, golf camps and golf outings to choose from. Most golf courses have a resident pro, or golf expert, who will give advice to new players.

On a **driving range**, golfers spend many hours practising how to stand and how to hold and swing the club to hit the ball.

Extra equipment

Golfers wear special gloves to provide grip, and shoes with spikes to stop them slipping as they take their shots. In their kit they also need golf balls and 'tees'. A tee is a small, Y-shaped piece of wood or plastic on which the ball sits when the player **tees off** at the start of each hole.

Having hit the ball, the player 'follows through' with a swing.

DID YOU KNOW?

Some golf courses that are next to the sea are called 'links'. One of the most famous is Pebble Beach (left) in California, USA. It overlooks the Pacific Ocean. In Ireland, Ballybunion is beside the Atlantic.

Hockey

HOCKEY in its modern form was first played in the mid 1700s by schoolchildren in England, and it is still popular with children. Play usually takes place on a rectangular field, where the players are arranged in similar positions to those on a football field – there are attackers, defenders and a goalkeeper. Using wooden sticks, the players pass the ball up and down the field and try to hit it into the other team's goal.

A team game

There are 11 players in a hockey team. As in football, **passing**, **marking** and **tackling** are important aspects of the game. The hockey stick itself is just under 1m long. It is similar to an ice-hockey stick, but the head – the area used to hit the ball – is smaller.

OLYMPIC ALL-STAR

Hockey has been part of the summer Olympic Games since 1908. One of the most successful players of all time is Rechelle Hawkes (above) of Australia. She has won three Olympic golds.

◀ A penalty corner is a type of play that allows one team to try and score from near the goal. They get this chance because the other team has fouled. Five players from the defending team must stand behind the back line until the ball has been hit.

STICK FACTS

The head of a hockey stick has a rounded side and a flat side. The flat side is used to hit the ball.

FIELD FACTS

Most outdoor hockey is played on artificial pitches that measure 91.4m long by 55m wide. The goal at each end is 2.14m high and 3.6m wide. Around the goal there is a D-shaped area known as the **shooting circle**.

Hockey involves a lot of tackling by opponents. Players are allowed to hit the ball only with the flat face of the stick.

Basic equipment

If you want to get started in hockey, you'll need shin pads, a stick and a ball. The shin pads are to protect the lower legs from the impact of the ball or another player's stick. In schools, hockey is often still played on grass, and studded boots will provide grip. At leisure centres and elsewhere, however, synthetic surfaces are more popular and trainers should be worn. Some hockey players also wear mouth guards to protect their teeth and goggles for their eyes.

Street hockey

Street hockey is closely related to hockey and ice hockey. It is basically the same game, but is played on paved surfaces such as a street or rollerblading rink. The players wear trainers or rollerblades, and use ice-hockey sticks instead of round-ended sticks.

ICE HOCKEY

Ice hockey is a fast-paced, exciting game similar to hockey, but played on ice with ice-hockey sticks and a puck (a smooth-sided, solid, thick disc). The players wear heavy pads and helmets to protect themselves from the sticks, the flying puck or a stray ice skate blade.

➤ There can be as many as 16 players in a street hockey team, but 10 of them will be reserves. Only six of the team take part in the action at any one time.

▶ *A flying hockey ball travels fast and is very hard, so the goalkeeper protects his or her body and face with extra padding and a helmet.*

INDOOR HOCKEY

In indoor hockey, the number of players, the rules of the game and the size of the field are all different from outdoor hockey. Instead of 11 players in a team, there are six. The players cannot hit the ball, as in outdoor hockey. Instead, they push, scoop or flick the ball towards or into the goal.

CRICKET is popular in many countries, especially the UK, India, Sri Lanka, South Africa, Pakistan, Australia and the West Indies. The rules are straightforward, and once you've mastered the basics it's a great game to play.

PROTECTIVE GEAR AND EQUIPMENT

A cricket ball is very hard, so most cricket players wear equipment to protect their hands, face and legs. The wicketkeeper, for instance, wears leg pads to protect his shins and heavy gloves to protect his hands. The batsmen wear helmets with face grills, arm guards, leg pads and gloves.

Playing the game

In cricket, two teams of 11 players take turns batting and fielding. The game is played on a field that includes a long, narrow section called the pitch. At each end of the pitch is a set of stumps and bails (an arrangement of three upright sticks topped by two smaller sticks) called a **wicket**. The batsman stands in front of the wicket and tries to hit the ball to prevent the bowler (on the other team) from hitting the wicket with the ball. A second batsman (on the same team as the first) stands by the bowler's wicket. To score a 'run', the batsman hitting the ball must run and change places with the other batsman.

Team effort

Other people on the field include fielders, two umpires (who enforce the rules) and the **wicketkeeper**. Each team's turn at the wicket is called an **innings**. The team that scores the most runs wins.

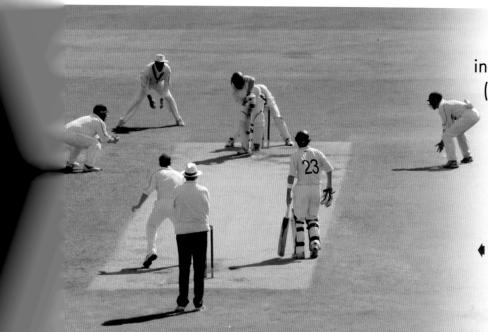

Bowlers try and make the ball hard to hit. Some balls are bowled very fast. Others bounce and curve in an unexpected direction.

TWENTY20 CRICKET

Twenty20 is a shortened form of cricket that takes about three hours to play. By comparison, a Test match – a game between two national teams – may take up to five days to complete. In Twenty20 cricket the players often wear brightly coloured clothes (instead of white).

◀ *A batsman uses a wooden (traditionally willow) paddle-like bat to defend the wicket.*

DID YOU KNOW?

A professional cricket ball weighs between 155.9g and 163g, about the same as an American baseball. Balls for children and women are smaller.

POOL

POOL is played on a rectangular table with pockets at the four corners and in the middle of each long side. Sixteen balls are used: seven red ones, seven yellow ones, a black ball and the white **cue ball**. Sometimes, instead, players use seven solid-coloured balls (numbered 1 to 7), the black 8-ball and seven striped balls (numbered 9 to 15). Using a stick called a cue, the player hits the white cue ball, which in turn knocks one of the other balls into a pocket.

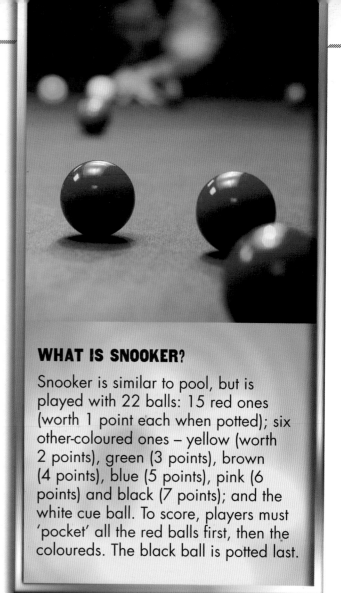

WHAT IS SNOOKER?

Snooker is similar to pool, but is played with 22 balls: 15 red ones (worth 1 point each when potted); six other-coloured ones – yellow (worth 2 points), green (3 points), brown (4 points), blue (5 points), pink (6 points) and black (7 points); and the white cue ball. To score, players must 'pocket' all the red balls first, then the coloureds. The black ball is potted last.

Cue clues

The cue is usually made of wood and is slightly thicker at one end. The narrow end has a leather tip, and is used to hit the white cue ball. Most pool players use chalk on the tip to improve contact between the stick and the ball.

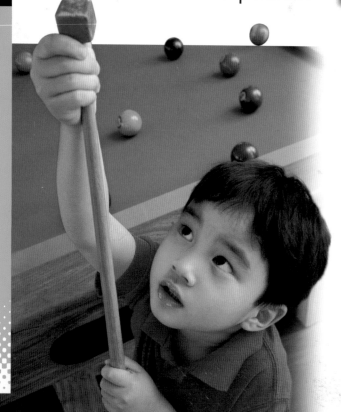

Chalking the leather tip of the pool cue helps the player to hit the ball with greater accuracy towards the hole, because it stops the cue from skidding off the ball.

Whose turn?

The players have one set of balls each – either a colour (the reds or yellows) or the spots or stripes. They each try to pot all their balls into the pockets before the other player. If a player pots the correct ball, he or she has another go. If he or she fails to pot a ball, the opponent has a turn. In most games, the black ball must be potted last.

▶ *To judge what angle and strength to hit the cue ball, it helps to look down the length of the cue so you can line up your shot.*

THE SPORT OF KINGS?

Many famous rulers, including Mary, Queen of Scots and Napoleon Bonaparte, loved playing billiards (from which snooker and pool were developed).

asphalt A smooth, tar-like surface.

base (first, second, third) Square markers used in baseball to mark three of the four points of the baseball diamond (home plate is the fourth.)

baseman A fielding position in baseball; the first baseman plays on first base, the second baseman on second base, etc.

catcher The player in baseball who catches the ball thrown by the pitcher.

coach An instructor who works with players to improve their game.

cue ball The white ball used to hit other balls in snooker and pool.

driving range A place for golfers to practise hitting and driving.

fielder A player whose job is to catch or stop the ball and return it.

game (tennis) A match is made up of a series of games. A game is won when one player, or pair, scores at least four points and is more than one point clear of the opponent(s). (The first point is called 15, the second is 30, the third is 40 and 40-all is called deuce. The next person to score has the 'advantage'. If the player with the advantage wins the next point, he or she wins the game. If he or she loses it, the score goes back to deuce.)

hole-in-one In golf, a shot that enters the hole from the tee.

home plate The base that baseball runners must reach to score a run.

home run A run scored by a baseball player who hits the ball so far that he or she is able to run around all four bases in one go before the ball is returned to base.

innings In cricket, each team's turn to bat at the wicket.

iron A type of golf club generally used for accurate shots taken between the tee and the green.

Little League A US organization that manages baseball and softball leagues for children around the world.

Major League Baseball The organization that oversees professional-level baseball in the USA and Canada.

marking When a player on one team stays close to a specific player on the other team, in order to make it difficult for him or her to pass or receive the ball.

Masters A major golf tournament played each year in the USA.

match (tennis) A tennis match consists of two or three sets. A set includes at least six games.

Open A competition (as in the US Open in golf and tennis) which nationally top-rated athletes, either amateur or professional, may enter.

out (baseball) The batter is out if he hits the ball and a fielder catches it before it hits the ground; if the first baseman catches the ball before the batter reaches first base; or if the pitcher throws the ball three times and the batter fails to hit it.

passing When a player hits or kicks the ball to another player.

pitcher The baseball player who throws, or pitches, the ball over the home plate towards the batter and the catcher. The batter tries to hit the ball before it reaches the catcher.

polo A game in which horse-riders use mallets to hit a ball into goal.

putter A flat-sided golf club used on the green to hit the ball into the hole.

rounders A game in which two teams of nine players take turns batting and fielding the ball, and running around four posts to score rounders.

run In baseball, when a player runs around all three bases and crosses the home plate. In cricket, when a batsman hits the ball and runs to the other wicket.

runner (baseball) Once the batter is on base, he or she becomes a runner.

set (tennis) A tennis match consists of two or three sets. To win a set, a player or team has to win at least six games, and at least two games more than their opponent(s) – for example, 6 games to 4 or 7 games to 5.

shooting circle The semicircular area in front of a hockey goal. Attempts at goal must be made from within the circle.

softball A game similar to baseball, but which uses a larger ball and a smaller diamond on the field.

tackling (hockey) When a player runs up to another player and places his or her hockey stick in the path of the ball to gain possession of it.

tee, tee off The tee is the space on a golf course from which the ball is struck (teed off) at the beginning of play for each hole.

wicket (cricket) Three upright poles (stumps) with two smaller sticks (bails) on top. There is a wicket at each end of the cricket pitch – the central strip where the batsmen run.

wicketkeeper (cricket) The player who stands behind the wicket and catches the ball bowled by the bowler (if the batsman does not hit it).

wood A type of golf club used to hit the ball off the tee or for long distances.

World Series The annual competition of two Major League Baseball teams.

WEBSITES
Lacrosse: www.laxlinks.com
www.bbc.co.uk/cbbc/sport/findasport
/lacrosse.shtml
Table Tennis: http://www.ittf.com/
games/game.htm
Baseball: www.baseballhalloffame.org